I0478642

Tough Guy

Humphrey Bogart in His Own Words
And in the Words of Those Who Knew Him

By Michael Turback
Author of *All the Gin Joints*

COPYRIGHT NOTICE

TOUGH GUY: Humphrey Bogart in His Own Words and in the Words of Those Who Knew Him is published and copyrighted © 2013 by History Company LLC (www.historycompany.com). All rights reserved. No part of this book may be reproduced in any form by any electronic or mechanical means (including photocopying, recording, or information storage or retrieval) without permission in writing from the publisher. Users are not permitted to mount any part of this book on the World Wide Web. Requests to the publisher for permission should be addressed to the Permissions Department, History Company LLC, support@historycompany.com

Limit of Liability/Disclaimer of Warranty: While the publisher and the author have used their best efforts in preparing this book, they make no representations or warranties with respect to the accuracy or completeness of the contents of this book and specifically disclaim any implied warranties of merchantability or fitness for a particular purpose. No warranty may be created or extended by sales representatives or written sales materials. The advice and strategies contained herein may not be suitable for your situation. Neither the publisher nor the author shall be liable for any loss of profit or any other commercial damages, including but not limited to special, incidental, consequential, or other damages.

The entries in this book have been drawn from many sources, and are assumed to be accurate as quoted in their previously published forms. Although every effort has been made to verify the quotes and sources, the publisher cannot guarantee their perfect accuracy.

History Company books are available at special discounts for bulk purchases (shipping and handling charges apply). For more information, contact:

History Company LLC
www.historycompany.com
(800) 891-0466

Printed in the United States of America.

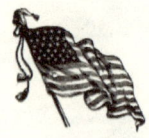

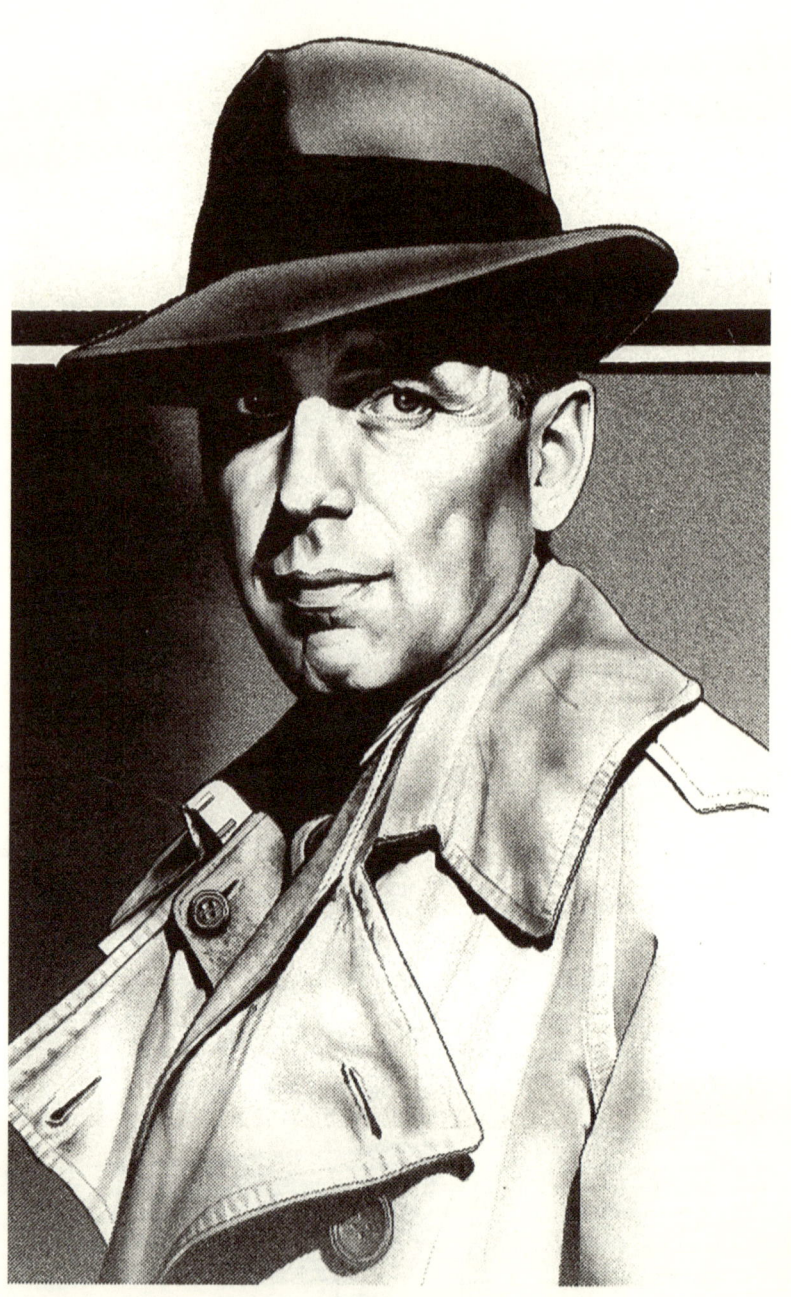

"Bogart is so much better than any other tough-guy actor that he makes bums of the [Alan] Ladds and the [Dick] Powells.... Bogart can be tough without a gun. Also, he has a sense of humor that contains that grating undertone of contempt. Ladd is hard, bitter, and occasionally charming, but he is after all a small boy's idea of a tough guy. Bogart is the genuine article."

— Raymond Chandler

Words Speak Louder

Whatever the "something special' is that constitutes a man's man and an actor's actor, he had it – and in abundance.

Raised by a genteel East Coast family with a doctor father and a well-known artist mother, Humphrey DeForest Bogart emerged from a minor theatrical career in the 1920s to become one of Hollywood's most distinctive leading men, typically cast as smart, playful, courageous, tough, occasionally reckless characters who lived in a world of dames, mugs, and coppers, yet anchored by a hidden moral code – hard-boiled cynics who ultimately show a noble side.

In *The Maltese Falcon*, when Sydney Greenstreet's Kasper Gutman, says to Bogart's Sam Spade, "By Gad, sir, you are a character – there's never any telling what you'll say or do next, except that it's bound to be something astonishing," he might just as well have been describing the real-life Humphrey Bogart. Here was a man who could charm the birds off the trees one minute, and tell a producer to go straight to hell the next. They threw away the mold when he moved on.

This fizzy cocktail of a book lifts the veil off the movie tough guy to reveal the real-life tough guy. It provides an unvarnished portrait of a hard-drinking, prankish extrovert whose heart was as soft as his screen lines were hard. You get a little history and a bit of sociology. But the fun comes from the abundant helping of irreverence. His contemporaries as well as subsequent observers have plenty to say about Bogie – the good, the bad, and the ugly – and his own brash words provide an affectionate, perceptive portrait of a marvelous, contradictory man.

Michael Turback
Citizen of the World

"Bogart was a medium-sized man, not particularly impressive off screen. Put him on camera, however, and those lights and shadows organized themselves into another nobler personality – heroic."

— John Huston

"I can't get in a mild discussion without turning it into an argument. There must be something in my tone of voice, or this arrogant face
– something that antagonizes everybody.
Nobody likes me on sight. I suppose that's
why I'm cast as the heavy."

— H.B.

"Like Edward G. Robinson when he was younger, all [Bogart] has to do to dominate a scene is enter it."

— Raymond Chandler

"I'm not good-looking. I used to be, but not anymore. Not like Robert Taylor. What I have got is I have character in my face. It's taken an awful lot of late nights and drinking to put it there. When I go to work in a picture, I say, 'Don't take the lines out of my face. Leave them there.'"

— H.B.

"His great basic quality was a splendid roughness. Even when perfectly groomed, I felt I could have lit a match on his jaw.'"

— Peter Ustinov

"There are only a few actors in the world you can have in every scene and not get tired of them. But I don't think you get tired of Bogart ."

— Howard Hawks

"I'm an old-fashioned, last century boy,
but don't let it get around. It could ruin my
reputation."

— H.B.

"He is the only man I have ever known who truly and completely belonged to himself.... His convictions about life, work and people were so strong they were unshakeable. Nothing – no one – could make him lower his standards, lessen his character. He had the greatest gifts a man could have: respect for himself, for his craft; integrity about life as well as work."

— Lauren Bacall

"I have politeness and manners. I was
brought up that way. But in this goldfish-bowl
life, it is sometimes hard to use them ."

— H.B.

"He was very friendly. Very easy. With life.
Very sensible. Horse sense especially. I think
he was sensitive. Just a really – nice – man.
And that's rare in our business."

— Katherine Hepburn

"Bogart was quite alarming to meet, for the first time, with his sardonic humor and his snarl that passed for a smile. It took me a little while to realize that he had perfected an elaborate camouflage to cover up one of the kindest and most generous of hearts."

— David Niven

"Bogie is in constant anxiety to be what he calls a character, to distinguish himself away from his occupation. He has never allowed his [own] character to develop. [He] would love nothing better than to be considered a character, even more than a good actor. [He] does not like his career and at the same time he is proud of it."

— Mike "Prince" Romanoff

"Humphrey was not a tough guy. He was not at all. He was about as tough as Little Lord Fauntleroy."

— Clifton Webb

"If a face like Ingrid Bergman's looks at you as though you're adorable, everybody does. You don't have to act very much."

— H.B.

"Who'd want to kiss Bogart?"

— Jack Warner

Bogie didn't have to kiss the girl. He didn't have to touch her. You knew by the way he looked at her."

— Mary Astor

[On making *Casablanca*] "I kissed him, but I never really knew him. He came out of his dressing room, did his scene, then fled away again. It was all very strange and distant."

— Ingrid Bergman

"I didn't do anything [in *Casablanca*] I've never done in twenty movies before that, and suddenly they discover I'm sexy. Any time that Ingrid Bergman looks at a man, he has sex appeal."

— H.B.

"[On love scenes] I don't like them, maybe because I don't do them very well. It isn't possible to shoot a love scene without having a hairy-chested group of grips standing four feet away from you, chewing tobacco.'"

— H.B.

"I made so many films which were more important, but the only one people ever want to talk about is that one with Bogart."

— Ingrid Bergman

[On the line, "Here's looking at you, kid"]
"What would that line have been without Bogie, coming out of the mouth of some other actor, any other actor? He lives forever saying that line."

— Julius Epstein

"I yield to no man in the animal magnetism field."

— H.B.

"Bogart didn't unburden himself to men. He loved to be in love and with a woman. I think he came closer to leveling with them than with anybody."

— John McClain

"Being supremely confident of his own attractiveness to women, he scorned every form of demonstrativeness."

— Louise Brooks

"The ladies like Bogie, but he was not a ladies man."

— John Huston

"I had had enough women by the time I was 27 to know what I was looking for in a wife the next time I married."

— H.B.

"The zipper was invented in 1926. Bogie demanded one be sewed into all of his pants – sex was a lot faster that way.'"

— Joan Blondell

[On his third wife Mayo Methot] "I like a jealous wife. And I like a good fight. So does Mayo. We have some first-rate battles."

— H.B.

"Their fights usually ended in bed."

— Mary Baker

"The Bogart-Methot marriage was the sequel to the Civil War."

— Julius Epstein

"Me hit a woman? Why I'm too sweet and chivalrous. Besides, it's dangerous.'"

— H.B.

"Bogie was an old-fashioned man. He kidded that a woman's place was in the home, but he was only half kidding. He had divorced three actresses and was convinced that a career and marriage don't mix."

— Lauren Bacall

"I always cry at weddings, especially my own."

— H.B.

"She [Lauren] matched his insolence. Betty came along at exactly the right time for Bogie. He was mature and she was a kid, and I think he had a ball showing her what life was all about."

— Bette Davis

[On Lauren Bacall] "She`s a real Joe. You'll fall in love with her like everybody else."

— H.B.

"He taught me how to live, that it was okay to trust. He taught me to keep going, no matter what. He did. And he is."

— Lauren Bacall

"She [Lauren] and Bogie seemed to have the most enormous opinion of each other's charms, and when they fought, it was with the utter confidence of two cats locked deliciously in the same cage."

— Katharine Hepburn

[In a letter to Lauren Bacall] "I will love you for the rest of my life, Baby"

— H.B.

"You had to stay awake married to him. Every time I thought I could relax and do everything I wanted, he'd buck. There was no way to predict his reactions, no matter how well I knew him."

— Lauren Bacall

[On Lauren Bacall] "She makes great scrambled eggs."

— H.B.

"He's the ugliest handsome man I've ever seen."

— Lauren Bacall

[On being a father] "What do you do with a kid? They don't drink."

— H.B.

[On son Stephen] "I guess maybe I had the kid too late in life. I just don't know what to do about him. But I love him. I hope he knows that ."

— H.B.

"I don't know that he had a lot of friends. I think Frank Sinatra was a friend. Huston was a friend. Richard Brooks was a friend. But really his off screen loves were chess, and his boat, which are both solitary ventures."

— Stephen Bogart

"Unless you really understand the water and understand the reason for being on it and understand the love of sailing and the feeling of quietness and solitude, you don't really belong on a boat anyway."

— H.B.

"Sailing – that was the part of him no one could get at. It wasn't anything materialistic. It was some kind of inner soul, an almost mystical hideaway."

— Truman Capote

[On his love of sailing] "The sea – the air –
It's clean and healthy and away from the
Hollywood gossip and leeches."

— H.B.

"The trouble with having dames on board [his boat Santana] is you can't pee over the side."

— H.B.

"An actor needs something to stabilize his personality, something to nail down what he really is, not what he is currently pretending to be."

— H.B.

[After moving to a mansion in Holmby Hills, an exclusive neighborhood between Beverly Hills and Bel Air] "We moved where all the creeps live."

— H.B.

"I was headstrong and he was patient and so loving and funny and witty…. a man of honor and integrity and he lived his life by the Ten Commandments and the Golden Rule. And, by golly, if anyone lied to him, they were out. Most of the time I was in awe of him; he was the most incredible man who walked on earth."

— Lauren Bacall

[When Lauren Bacall introduced him to her large extended family] "Christ, you've got more goddamn relatives than I've ever seen."

— H.B.

"Bogie didn't really enjoy food – he only ate to stay alive."

— Mike "Prince" Romanoff

"A hotdog at the ballpark is better than a steak at the Ritz."

— H.B.

"'I prefer to play chess rather than poker because no one can cheat.'"

— H.B.

"Bogie was never wrong about people. If he thought a person was all right, the person was all right. And if he thought a person was a phony, the person was a phony."

— Sam Jaffe

"I don`t approve of the John Waynes and the Gary Coopers saying 'Shucks, I ain't no actor – I'm just a bridge builder or a gas station attendant.' If they aren`t actors, what the hell are they getting paid for? I have respect for my profession. I worked hard at it."

— H.B.

"The phrase 'movie star' is misused so much that it has no real meaning any more. Any little pinhead who makes one picture is called a star. To be a star you have to drag your weight in the box office and be recognized wherever you go."

— H.B.

"Bogart could have been color blind. He got to know a man before he decided if he liked him or not."

— Sammy Davis Jr.

"He liked a good time, he liked booze and whatnot; one of the nicest men that I ever met in my life. I don't think he had any prejudice so far as race was concerned. He was just like an ordinary guy, even though he was a big star, just an ordinary guy at heart. That's the way he lived."

— Allan McMillan

"Joan Crawford – no matter how much I can't stand the lady – is a star."

— H.B.

[On Bette Davis] "Even when I was carrying a gun, she scared the bejesus out of me."

— H.B.

"I think Marlon Brando is one of the best young actors in the business, and I think he'll be great as soon as he gets that potato out of his mouth."

— H.B.

"I came out here with one suit and everybody said I looked like a bum. Twenty years later Marlon Brando came out with only a sweat-shirt and the town drooled over him. That shows how much Hollywood has progressed."

— H.B.

[On Katharine Hepburn] "She talks at you as though you were a microphone; she lectured the hell out of me on temperance and the evils of drink. She doesn`t give a damn how she looks. I don`t think she tries to be a character. I think she is one."

— H.B.

[On George Raft] "He reads every line the same way. One two three pause. One two three pause. How do you compete against that?"

— H.B.

[On Myra Loy's tip-tilted nose] "It's one of the world's greatest treasures."

— H.B.

[On Audrey Hepburn] "She's okay if you don't mind 20 takes."

— H.B.

"Bogie hated learning lines. He knew every trick in the book to fuck up a scene and get a retake if he felt a scene wasn't going his way."

— Ava Gardner

[On Spencer Tracy] "After me, he's the best."

— H.B.

[On Frank Sinatra] "I don't think Frank's an adult emotionally. He can't settle down."

— H.B.

[On William Holden] "The guy is a dumb prick."

— H.B.

[On Lew Ayres] "He is prettier than most gals I know. Put some lipstick on him and a dress and I'd go for him myself."

— H.B.

[On agent and producer Sam Jaffe] "I trust Sam more than anyone else in the world."

— H.B.

"If you want to get [John Huston] roused, tell him something that appeals to his sense of justice or courage."

— H.B.

[On John Huston] "Risk, action, and making the best use of what's around is what makes him tick."

— H.B.

"Huston has more color and is more photogenic than 90 per cent of the actors in Hollywood."

— H.B.

"Do I subscribe to the Laurence Olivier school of acting? Ah, nuts. I'm an actor. I just do what comes naturally."

— H.B.

"Acting is experience with something sweet behind it."

— H.B.

"Acting is like sex: you either do it and don't talk about it, or you talk about it and don't do it. That's why I'm always suspicious of people who talk too much about either."

— H.B.

"An actor needs something to stabilize his personality, something to nail down what he really is, not what he is currently pretending to be."

— H.B.

"The only thing you owe the public is a good performance."

— H.B.

[After viewing *In Which We Serve*] "Obviously, Noel Coward is the guy Orson Welles thinks he is."

— H.B.

[On the untrained beefcake stars of the early 1950s, many of them picked up for screen tests from sidewalks and gas stations] "Shout 'gas' around the studios today, and half the young male stars will come running."

— H.B.

"He wasn't extremist in anything, except telling the truth. You had to admire Bogie. He always said what he thought. "Goddamit,' he used to say, 'if you don't want to hear the truth, don't ask me.'"

— Lauren Bacall

"All over Hollywood, they are continually advising me 'Oh, you mustn't say that. That will get you in a lot of trouble' when I remark that some picture or writer or director or producer is no good. I don't get it. If he isn't any good, why can't you say so? If more people would mention it, pretty soon it might start having some effect."

— H.B.

"Bogart thought of himself as Scaramouch, the mischievous scamp who sets off the fireworks, then nips out."

— Nunnally Johnson

"I had heard rumors that he was wild and crazy and a drinker and a swearer – and he was! But he was gentle…. against swearing when I was around."

— Joan Leslie

"Here was a man who read. He had breeding. People think he was just a drunk and that all he did was have fights. But he always surrounded himself with writers – he admired writing. In that respect he was a lot different than most actors."

— Sam Jaffe

"A good actor is supposed to 'lose himself' in the character he plays. Instead the character got lost in Bogie, and gained by it.... His precision timing was no accident, and he kept other actors on their toes because he listened to them during a scene, he watched, he looked at them. He wasn't up stage center acting all by himself.... he 'related.'"

— Mary Astor

"I'm known as a guy who always squawks about roles, but never refuses to play one. I've never forgotten a piece of advice Holbrook Blinn gave me when I was a young squirt and asked him how I could get a reputation as an actor. He said, 'Just keep working.' The idea is that if you're always busy, sometime someone is going to get the idea that you must be good."

— H.B.

"He always had time for the usual chit-chat between takes, but anybody who led himself to believe that Bogie never worked on his parts was terribly mistaken. He never did any role without serious thinking about every phase of the character he played."

— Leonid Kinsky

"If it's a louse-heel [role], give it to Bogart"

— Vincent Sherman

"I made more lousy pictures than any actor in history."

— H.B.

[On making *The Return of Doctor X*] "If it'd been Jack Warner's blood, I wouldn't have minded so much. The trouble was they were drinking mine and I was making this stinking movie."

— H.B.

[On *Swing Your Lady*] "The worst picture I ever made."

— H.B.

[On screen love] "I have absolutely no interest in who gets the girl. I don't care. I don't see any reason to spend two hours to see who gets the girl especially since you know who's going to get her from the beginning – usually the actor who gets the most money."

— H.B.

[On *The Petrified Forest*] "It marked my deliverance from the ranks of the sleek, sybaritic, stiff-shirted, swallow-tailed 'smoothies' to which I seemed condemned to life."

— H.B.

"He could get into a minor twitch of the mouth the force of a slug from an automatic."

— James Agee

"When it came to fighting, Bogart was about as tough as Shirley Temple."

— James Cagney

"I have absolutely no use for Communism nor for anyone who serves that philosophy."

— H.B.

[On the House Un-American Activities Committee] "They'll nail anyone who ever scratched his ass during the National Anthem."

— H.B.

[About himself] "Democrat in politics, Episcopalian by upbringing, dissenter by disposition."

— H.B.

[On homosexuality] "I say if it feels good, go for it. It's no one's goddamn business but your own."

— H.B.

[To Noel Coward] "Noel, I have to tell you that if I had my druthers and I liked guys you would be the one I'd want to be with. But, unfortunately, I like girls."

— H.B.

[To Jackie Gleason] "You look like the man who came to dinner – and ate the guests.'"

— H.B.

"He was devilish if he thought you were a phony. Like a cat with a mouse, he'd never let you off."

— Katherine Hepburn

[On Warner Brothers] "This studio has more suspensions than the Golden Gate Bridge."

— H.B.

"The people with power loved you as long as you could make a dollar for them. After that, you were gone – they wiped you off the slate. You never existed."

— H.B.

"I don't hurt the industry. The industry hurts itself, by making so many lousy movies – as if General Motors deliberately put out a bad car."

— H.B.

"John Huston is the only real genius in Hollywood, a real poet."

— H.B.

[To Bogart, on casting *The African Queen*]
"The hero is a lowlife, and you are the biggest lowlife in town and therefore most suitable for the part"

— John Huston

"A good director is like a good psychiatrist. He builds up the confidence of his players until they forget their fears and inhibitions. Once you have that confidence [in a director], you're not afraid to take chances."

— H.B.

[On John Huston] "He's just a mite teched with genius. You have to be a mite teched to be a genius, I guess."

— H.B.

[On Howard Hughes] "He is the weirdest, most God-awful creature ever to set foot in Hollywood."

— H.B.

"My parents fought. We kids would pull the covers over our ears to keep out the sound of fighting. Our home was kept together for the sake of the children as well as for the sake of propriety."

— H.B.

[On his mother] "She was essentially a woman who loved work, loved her work, to the exclusion of everything else. I don't think she honestly cared about anything but her work and her family. Yet she was totally incapable of showing affection to us."

— H.B.

"If, when I was grown up, I [had] sent my mother one of those Mother's Day telegrams or said it with flowers, she would have returned the wire and flowers to me, collect."

— H.B.

"I can't say I ever loved my mother, I admired her."

— H.B.

"He was definitely a man's man, but he treated women with respect. He didn't have an entourage or a driver or any of that stuff."

— Stephen Bogart

"Bogie is fanatically independent, yet he can't stand being alone."

— Lauren Bacall

[On serving in the Navy during World War I]
"At 18, war was great stuff. Paris! French girls! Hot damn! The war was a big joke."

— H.B.

"The only good reason to have money is so that you can tell any SOB in the world to go to hell.'"

— H.B.

"You're crazy if you think you'll make a hero out of him – the son of a bitch lisps!"

— Tay Garnett

"Fame comes with its own standard. A guy who twitches his lips is just another guy with a lip twitch – unless he's Humphrey Bogart."

— Sammy Davis Jr.

[On working with Rod Steiger in *The Harder They Fall*] "These Actor's Studio types – they mumble their lines. I can't hear their words. I miss the cues. This scratch-your-ass-and-mumble school of acting doesn't please me."

— H.B.

"Bogart has endured because in our society the family unit has gone to pieces. And here you had a guy about whom there was no doubt. There is no doubt that he is the leader. There is no doubt that he is the strong one. There is no doubt with this man that he can handle himself, that he can protect the family. This is all unconscious, but with Bogart you are secure, you never doubt that he will take care of things."

— Rod Steiger

"I've worked with a lot of big actors. Most of them were worried how they looked more than anything else, and they wouldn't play the character. But with Bogart, every time was a characterization. He'd play to you, not to some camera over there. And he expected you to play to him."

— Aldo Nadi

"He was completely honest – a rarity among actors. He didn't turn his charm on and off. You took him as he was."

— Irene Manning

"I don't think there was ever a point at which he was acting a line, where he was reading the line for effect. Some actors have tricks in reading. Others, like Bogie and Tracy, never resort to tricks. There was always a newness, and a freshness."

— Edward Dmytryk

"He had an aura of his own. When he walked out there, you were dealing with a star, and you knew it. He had such an inner strength."

— Irving Moore

"Scotch is a very valuable part of my life"

— H.B.

[On making *The African Queen*] "I built a solid wall of scotch between me and the bugs. If a mosquito bit me, he'd fall over dead drunk."

— H.B.

"I went on the wagon just once. It was the most miserable afternoon of my life "

— H.B.

[On the Rat Pack] "Rats are very well behaved, but they are also for staying up late and drinking lots of booze."

— H.B.

"Who isn't [drunk] at 3 o'clock in the morning? So we get stiff once in a while. This is a free country isn't it?"

— H.B.

"Errol Flynn and I are the only ones left who do any good old hell-raising."

— H.B.

"A good drinker can get absolutely stiff and the fellow next to him doesn't know it. You had to handle it, it shouldn't handle you.

— H.B.

"Sober, Bogart was great. Drunk, he was a dirty bastard."

— Allen Rivkin

[Explaining a hangover] "I chose this Oxford gray suit to go with my complexion."

— H.B.

"You got to hand it to him. When he gets barred, he gets barred from all the right places."

— Lauren Bacall

"You don't get to be the Boris Karloff of the supper clubs overnight. You've got to work at it."

— H.B.

"I don't trust a bastard who doesn't drink.
They're afraid of revealing their true selves."

— H.B.

"Bogie had an alcoholic thermostat. He just set his thermostat at noon, pumped in some scotch, and stayed at a nice even glow all day, re-dosing as necessary."

— Nunnally Johnson

"I do as I damned please. I defend my right to cut a caper if I feel like it"

— H.B.

"Bogie's hospitality went far beyond food and drink. He fed a guest's spirit as was well as his body, plied him with good will until he became drunk in the heart as well as his legs."

— John Huston

"Bogart had everything – excellent background; stage experience, which Howard [Hawks] was in awe of; humble, didn't have airs. An ordinary guy. But a professional. And on the set, in spite of the drinking."

— Dee Hawks Cramer

"The problem with the world is that everyone is a few drinks behind. If everyone in the world would take three drinks, we would have no trouble. If Stalin, Truman and everybody else in the world had three drinks right now, we'd all loosen up and we wouldn't need the United Nations."

— H.B.

"Bogart's a hell of a nice guy until around 11:30 PM. After that, he thinks he's Bogart."

— Dave Chasen

"Bogart is a first-class person with an obsessive compulsion to behave like a second-class person."

— Mike "Prince" Romanoff

"Bogie loved to raise hell. Of a completely harmless nature. I mean he loved to cause ructions and make noises – almost like a little boy, that was. You know, beating the drum, marching around the room. You see a kid doing this."

— John Huston

"His big kick was to get people drunk.
I felt it was a kind of sadistic way to spend
an evening."

— Max Wilk

"He was either charming or belligerent, but his belligerence was never against somebody who was either bigger or stronger or more mentally powerful. He would come in and be sweet and charming and then find somebody who looked weak and defenseless and get him."

— Cynthia Lindsay

"I examine your face, Bogie, your ugly face, and I know that somewhere underneath the sickening face of a shit – is a real shit."

— Billy Wilder

"He wasn't a man that unmasked easily."

— Ida Lupino

"Bogie looked at the world, at his place in it, at movies, at life in general, and there was something about it that made him sick, contemptuous, bitter. And it showed. He related to people as though they had no clothes on, and no skin for that matter."

— Mary Astor

"For all his outward toughness, insolence, braggadocio, and contempt (and those were always part of the character he played, though they were not entirely within Bogie), there came through a kind of sadness, loneliness and heartbreak (all of which were very much part of Bogie the man). I always felt sorry for him – sorry that he imposed upon himself the facade of the character with which he had become identified."

— Edward G. Robinson

[On the 1952 Oscars] "I don't think I have a chance. For one thing, I don't have a big studio behind me to do the campaigning. And there are some pretty sharp boys in the race."

— H.B.

[On Academy Awards] "The only honest way to find the best actor would be to let everybody play Hamlet and let the best man win. Of course, you'd get some pretty funny Hamlets that way."

— H.B.

[After winning the Oscar for Best Actor in *The African Queen*] "The best way to survive an Oscar is to never try to win another one. You've seen what happens to some Oscar winners. They spend the rest of their lives turning down scripts while searching for the great role to win another one. Hell, I hope I'm never even nominated again. It's meat-and-potato roles for me from now on.'"

— H.B.

"His moral code was strict, and was based on, and almost indistinguishable from, the Ten Commandments. He didn't always obey them, but he believed in them."

— Nat Benchley

"Things are never so bad they can't be made worse.'"

— H.B.

"People who live in glass houses need ear plugs and a sense of humor. When I chose to be an actor I knew I'd be working in the spotlight. I also knew that the higher a monkey climbs the more you can see of his tail. So I keep my sense of humor and go right on leading my life and enjoying it. I wouldn't trade places with anybody."

— H.B.

"Bogart has a peculiar sense of humor. It is both impish and sadistic."

— Billy Wilder

"I use to have to look at the newspapers to find out what I'd been in the week before.'"

— H.B.

"There was a period in American history when you couldn't pick up a goddamned magazine without seeing my kisser in it."

— H.B.

[On movie fan magazines] "They are the damnedest bilge. They distort everything. I can't stand them. They build up an audience of people who read fan magazines."

— H.B.

"You're not a star until they can spell your name in Karachi."

— H.B.

[On publicity] "As long as they spell your name right and you are not accused of dope or rape, you are all right."

— H.B.

"I've been around a long time. Maybe the people like me."

— H.B.

"When the heavy, full of crime and bitterness, grabs his wounds and talks about death and taxes in a husky voice, the audience is his and his alone."

— H.B.

"Don't ever name a restaurant after me."

— H.B.

"In a film whose title perfectly defined Humphrey's own isolation among people, *In a Lonely Place* gave him a role that he could play with complexity because the film character's, the screenwriter's, pride in his art, his selfishness, his drunkenness, his lack of energy stabbed with lightning strokes of violence, were shared equally by the real Bogart."

— Louise Brooks

"It just always seemed to me as though he were permanently lonely. It gave him a rather poetic quality."

— Truman Capote

"I'm a professional. I've done pretty well, don't you think? I've survived in a pretty rough business."

— H.B.

[On aging] "I'm held together with platinum wire, glue, and hair tonic I take internally. I'm well preserved, don't you think, for an old guy?"

— H.B.

"When a man is sick, you get to know him. You find out whether he's made of soft wood or hard wood. I began to get fonder of Bogie with each visit. He was made of very hard wood indeed."

— Dr. Maynard Brandsma

"What's everybody whispering about? It's a respectable disease – nothing to be ashamed of, like something I might have had. The way people act, you'd think that cancer was as bad as VD."

— H.B.

[On reports of his illness] "What are the ghouls saying about me now? That I am fighting for my life in a hospital that doesn't exist out here; that my heart has stopped and been replaced by an old gasoline pump from a defunct Standard Oil station. I have been on the way to practically every cemetery you can name from here to the Mississippi – including several where I am certain they only accept dogs. All of the above upsets my friends, not to mention the insurance companies.'"

— H.B.

"I hate funerals. They aren't for the guy who's dead. They're for the guys who are left alive and enjoy mourning."

— H.B.

"I should never have switched from scotch to martinis."

— H.B. (his last words)

"No one who sat in his presence in the final weeks could ever forget. It was a unique display of sheer animal courage…. [I was] proud to be there, proud to be his friend, the friend of such a brave man."

— John Huston

"He never said, 'Why me?' None of the self-pitying stuff. He just took it."

— Joe Hyams

"The great thing about our marriage is whenever he wanted to teach me, he said, 'Long after I'm gone you'll remember me."

— Lauren Bacall

"I was crazy about Bogart. I used to follow him around and do what he did. I'd watch how he'd light his cigarette, what he drank."

— Frank Sinatra

"Bogart was an exceptional character in a sphere where characters are not usually exceptional."

— Peter Ustinov

"He was a man of enormous bark and absolutely no bite."

— David Niven

"Bogie was a fine person and a superb actor. He will be sorely missed in Hollywood.'"

— Bing Crosby

"He was one of the biggest guys I ever met. He walked straight down the center of the road. No maybes. Yes or no. He liked to drink. He drank. He liked to sail a boat. He sailed a boat. He was an actor. He was happy and proud to be an actor."

— Katherine Hepburn

"He was a man who tried very hard to be bad because he knew it was easier to get along in the world that way."

— Peter Bogdanovich

"He had a kind of eighteenth-century Alexander Pope nature. I think he would have made a superb Gatsby. His life reflected Gatsby's sense of being an outsider."

— Joseph Mankiewicz

"Like all really great stars, he had a secret. You never really know him altogether. He also had boldness of mind, freedom of thought – a buccaneer."

— George Cukor

"He had a protective shell of seeming indifference. He wasn't, but he did a lot of acting off-stage. He liked to act tough, liked to talk out of the side of his mouth."

— Chester Morris

"The three actors I admire the most are all dead. Humphrey Bogart, Spencer Tracy and the French actor, Jean Gabin. They're all very natural, sort of masculine without being overly macho."

— Michael Caine

"I think it's probably honest to say that there's a certain powerful stillness that I remember admiring tremendously as I grew up. And that would be Spencer Tracy... and Bogart and that particular approach to the work. The stillness, the economy, the grace of that work, so they would have been then, my heroes on the screen."

— Ben Kingsley

"I think all those actors from that generation, like Bogart – they were wonderful actors. They didn't act. They just came on and they did it, and the characters were wonderful."

— Anthony Hopkins

"His clenched jaw indubitably reminds us of the grin of a cheerful corpse, the last expression of a man who is about to die laughing."

— Francois Truffaut

"He was much more than an actor. He was an image of our condition. His face was a living reproach."

— Nicholas Ray

"He achieved class through his integrity and his devotion to what he thought was right. He believed in being direct, simple, and honest, all on his own terms, and this ruffled some people and endeared him to others."

— Nathaniel Benchley

"Bogart would have hated to be characterized as an intellectual. That was somehow for him a sign of weakness. Yet his logical approach to performance was very thorough and deep. He was one hell of an actor, and even though acting well was everything to him, he swept his accomplishment aside like it was nothing. He wanted to be sure nobody thought that he worked or took it seriously."

— Stanley Kramer

"He was an old fashioned man, a great romantic. And very emotional. He would cry when a dog died."

— Lauren Bacall

"Bogie was a hard-working guy, a good crafts-man. I have heard people say he wasn't really a good actor. I don't go along with that. His technical skill was quite brilliant. We who knew him well, we liked him. Bogie was for real."

— Mary Astor

"He was a tough man who found the world more corrupt than he had hoped. He invented the Bogart character and imposed it on a world impatient of men more obviously good. And it fitted his deceptive purpose like a glove."

— Alistair Cooke

"He wasn't tough, not really. He was, to me, a non-conformist. He had a cynicism without being unhealthy. He had a great curiosity and an arch kind of skepticism."

— Adlai Stevenson

"Himself, he never took too seriously – his work most seriously. He regarded the somewhat gaudy figure of Bogart, the star, with an amused cynicism; Bogart, the actor, he held in deep respect. He is quite irreplaceable. There will never be another like him."

— John Huston

An Invitation

With a view to future revisions, suggestions for additions,
corrections of errors, or other changes are invited.

The publishers cordially invite you to submit your criticisms
of this book and any other volumes that bear the History
Company name. Ideas for new books or reprints to be add-
ed to our catalogue are also most welcome.

Please address your criticisms, corrections, or suggestions
to: support@historycompany.com

www.ingramcontent.com/pod-product-compliance
Lightning Source LLC
Chambersburg PA
CBHW030928180526
45163CB00002B/498